Weirdest Buildings
of the West Country

Robert Hesketh

Bossiney Books • Exeter

The interior of the Rainforest Biome at the Eden Project

The photo on the title page is of Shute Barton gatehouse in East Devon, a National Trust property which is a fine example of Elizabethan design putting what would once have been defensive features to ornamental use

This reprint 2023
First published 2018 byBossiney Books Ltd,
68 Thorndale Courts, Whitycombe Way, Exeter, EX4 2NY
www.bossineybooks.com
ISBN 978-1-915664-13-6

Acknowledgements
The photograph on page 21 is by Matt Devenish.
All other photographs are by the author – www.roberthesketh.co.uk
or from the publishers' own collection.

Printed in Great Britain by R Booth Ltd, Penryn, Cornwall

Cornwall

The Egyptian House, Penzance

Penzance's extravagant Egyptian House (see cover photo) was built in 1835, riding the wave of enthusiasm for things Egyptian that began with Napoleon's Egyptian Campaign, followed by Nelson's defeat of the French at the Battle of the Nile (1798). Originally it was a museum and geological shop built for local collector John Lavin and is similar to P F Robinson's Egyptian Hall in Piccadilly, London and to John Foulston's Egyptian House in Devonport (page 22). It is probable that Foulston designed the Penzance house, but no one is certain.

If Lavin wanted an eye-catching shop-front he certainly got one. With its flamboyant and eclectic mix of Egyptian symbols, including lotus columns and Amon sundisks, the Egyptian House is about as far from the symmetry and restraint of most architecture of the period as it is possible to imagine. It is also very much an Englishman's idea of what an Egyptian house should look like and is crowned with the Hanoverian Royal Coat of Arms and an eagle.

Sadly neglected by the 1960s, the Egyptian House was then refurbished by architect Paul Pearn of Plymouth. After stripping back layers of paint from the elaborate Coade stone mouldings, Pearn decided the present colour scheme of brown and cream was closest to the original. The house's three apartments were fully restored by the Landmark Trust and are available for rent.
Egyptian House, 6 and 7 Chapel Street, Penzance TR18 4 AJ.
Landmark Trust, 01628 825925

Carn Brea Castle

Carn Brea Castle as we see it today is an 18/19th century hunting lodge in the form of a folly castle, complete with four castellated rectangular turrets, topped with chimneys. It is built on – and appears to melt into – a very irregular foundation of naturally outcropping granite. Thus the floors are on varying levels.

The wealthy Bassets of Tehidy, who owned many local mines, built it in the then fashionable Gothick style, incorporating some masonry from the earlier medieval building that existed here. This is considered to have been a chapel, built in 1379 and probably dedicated – like the chapel on Roche Rock (page 8) – to St Michael.

Now restored as a restaurant, the Castle is within Carn Brea's extensive Neolithic enclosure, which was later re-used as an Iron Age hillfort and offers a huge panorama stretching to both coasts. Like the nearby 27 m (90 ft) tall Basset monument, it is a prominent landmark. A record from 1898 shows that Carn Brea Castle was used as a beacon for ships and stipulated that the tenant showed a light in the north-facing window.

Carn Brea Restaurant, TR16 6SL, 01209 218358. Vehicle access is via a narrow lane, signed CARN BREA CASTLE *from Carnkie. This becomes a rough track with equally rough parking.*

Veryan roundhouses

Veryan is a beautiful village in Roseland, noted for its five roundhouses. They were built between 1815 and 1818 by Lostwithiel builder Hugh Rowe for the Revd Jeremiah Trist, squire and parson of the village. Constructed of rubble stone and cob, four have thatched roofs surmounted by crosses and are located in two pairs. One pair stands at the entrance to Veryan Green and the other pair at the opposite (southern) end of the village, on Pendower Road. However, the fifth, Beehive Cottage in the centre of Veryan behind the school, is slated.

Reputedly the five houses were built circular so that the Devil would have no corner to hide in, but more probably it was economical to build them like that. It is also claimed they were for Revd Trist's five daughters, but this is unlikely as one died before they were built and they were occupied by Trist's tenants or labourers.

Trist had been inspired by a round cottage built for a modest £42 at St Winnow near Lostwithiel by his friend Charles Vinnicombe Penrose, who published its floor plan in 1811. Revd Trist was obviously a man of means and a building enthusiast: he also had many other cottages constructed for his workers as well as two schools and a mansion, Parc Behan, for himself. This stands between the main part of the village and Veryan Green.

Veryan is signed from the A3078 St Mawes road. Please note that the roundhouses are not open to the general public, but two can be rented as holiday cottages

The Eden Project

The biomes at the Eden Project , futuristic in appearance, but practical in design and materials, were opened to the public in 2001. They are built in a landscaped former clay quarry and seem to emerge organically from the Earth.

The larger of the two, the Tropical Biome, is arrestingly massive. Covering 1.56 ha (3.9 acres), it houses the largest rainforest in captivity. It is 55 m (180 ft) high and accommodates a wide range of tropical trees and plants, including coffee, rubber, banana and giant bamboo. Temperature and humidity are maintained at rainforest levels year round. The smaller, but still vast, Mediterranean Biome also has its temperature and humidity regulated. It covers 0.65 ha (1.6 acres) and is tall enough (35 m or 115 ft) to house full size trees from the world's warm temperate zones, such as palms and olives, plus a host of smaller specimens, including grape vines.

The biomes are built of hundreds of hexagonal and pentagonal inflated plastic cells. These are supported solely by tubular steel frames. Rather than imitate the Crystal Palace which was built for London's Great Exhibition of 1851 and employed glass, architect Nicholas Grimshaw used the thermoplastic ETFE for the external cladding panels, the largest of which are 9 m (29.5 ft) across. As well as being much lighter than glass, this thermoplastic is safer – it doesn't shatter – and has other advantages.

Created from several thin layers of UV-transparent ETFE film, the cladding panels are inflated, making a huge insulating cushion. Although the panels are vulnerable to puncture, they can be easily repaired with special ETFE tape. This thermoplastic resists most stains, which simply wash off in the rain. Those that remain can be cleaned by abseiling teams.

Among Eden's millions of visitors are many students (some taking their degrees through the Project) and school groups. They are catered for in Eden's education facility, the Core. Grimshaw collaborated with Devon sculptor Peter Randall-Page in designing the copper clad roof of the building. They based the design on 'opposing spirals', the mathematical basis of plant growth seen in plants from pine cones to pineapples.

Eden is run as an educational charity and aims to connect people with one another and the living world. Tim Smit, the Project's co-founder explained in a video: 'Our aim was to regenerate, to create a symbol of optimism… We are part of Nature, not apart from Nature. I hope that by looking at the world through the lens of plants we can take you on a journey that – while it is about science and the natural world – is essentially about the most important species on it, humans…'

Roche Rock Chapel

Roche Rock is a dramatic outcrop of granite standing 20 m (66 ft) above the mid-Cornish plateau. Perched on top and built into the rock face, is the ruined chapel of St Michael. Dedicated in 1409, it has two storeys: a lower room for a chaplain or hermit, with the chapel above. Raising the granite blocks was a remarkable feat of medieval engineering.

It has been a ruin for at least 250 years, but the reason why it was built remains a mystery. It may have been built in imitation of St Michael's Mount opposite Marazion, or have served as a waymark and station for pilgrims on their way west to the Mount. One unsubstantiated tradition is that a hermit lived here, attended by his daughter.

Roche Rock has a part in the Tristan and Iseult tale. Legend also has it that the Rock is the refuge after death of wicked Jan Tregeagle, a harsh 17th century magistrate and steward for the Duchy of Cornwall. After his death, a guilty defendant called upon Tregeagle's spirit to witness for him. Tregeagle materialised to witness for the prosecution. Justice was done, but the court sentenced Tregeagle to the impossible task of emptying Dozmary Pool with a limpet shell. He fled to Roche Rock and haunts it to this day.

Access by (muddy) footpath. Park in marked bay by Roche church.

Lanhydrock gatehouse

Lanhydrock's wonderfully ornate gatehouse was completed in 1651 for Lord John Robartes, 1st Earl Radnor and Viscount Bodmin, whose family had grown wealthy in trade, enabling them to buy and extend Lanhydrock House from 1620. The gatehouse's octagonal towers are surmounted by crenellated parapets and obelisks, linked by a carriage arch. The upper storey has fine mullion windows, but the lower storey has more military looking cross-loops.

Despite the very recent Civil War, the gatehouse was built as a statement of wealth and social prestige, not for defence. This is perhaps surprising as Lord Robartes had served as a Parliamentarian commander and experienced the trauma of Lanhydrock being captured and his family held prisoner by Royalist forces under Sir Richard Grenville in 1644. By 1651, Robartes was in retirement and the war over, but to commemorate Parliament's victory, he planted a fine avenue of sycamores leading to his gatehouse. This was converted to a double beech avenue in the early 19th century. Happily the gatehouse survived the terrible fire of 1881. This destroyed much of the house, which was rebuilt in Victorian style.

Lanhydrock house and gardens are open through the National Trust.
PL30 5AD   01208 265950

Huer's Hut, near Towan Head, Newquay

The Huer's Hut is perched high on the cliff just east of Towan Head, commanding an excellent view of Newquay Bay. It provided shelter for generations of huers. Huers were watchmen who scanned the sea for shoals of fish, especially pilchard, which arrived in vast numbers and were once the mainstay of the Cornish fishing industry. Every fishing port once had its huer. On sighting a shoal – indicated by the disturbance and changed colour of the sea – he would alert the fishermen by crying Hevva! Hevva! through his long trumpet. The pubs emptied and dinner was left untasted as every able-bodied person rushed to man the boats. At one Cornish funeral in 1833, only the parson, the sexton and the deceased were left in church after the huer's cry was heard.

Once at sea, the fishermen looked to the huer to direct them with his semaphore-like signals made of two 'bushes' – originally furze bushes covered in cloth. Sometimes the bushes were also used to signal important news to men at sea, such as births and deaths. Wilkie Collins, the 19th century novelist, thought the huer would look like 'a maniac of the most dangerous character' to the uninitiated, but to the local community he was vital. Huers were well-paid and respected and their office was traditionally handed down from father to son. The task required concentration, keen sight and excellent knowledge of wind, weather and the movements of the fish. The stone-built Newquay hut has stood the test of time, whilst many wooden huers' huts have disappeared. Of special note are its massive chimney, its battlements and the external stair to the roof, where the huer stood when signalling to men at sea. The Newquay hut probably dates from the late 18th or early 19th century, but with medieval elements. It may have once served as a shelter for the person who lit a beacon guiding vessels into port.

King Edward Crescent, Newquay TR7 1EN

King Arthur's Great Halls, Tintagel

Trevena House, the façade of King Arthur's Great Halls, is a large, solid, dull Victorian granite building. Within, however, is another world, a remarkable feat of romantic imagination. The legendary realm of King Arthur and the Knights of the Round Table is given form and substance in finely carved granite and oak, in huge paintings and, above all, in some of the finest stained glass windows made in the 20th century.

The Halls were the brainchild of retired London entrepreneur, Arthurian enthusiast and Freemason, Frederick Thomas Glasscock. Combining a strong idealistic streak with the drive and ruthless practicality which had made him a fortune in the dried custard and confectionery business, Glasscock demanded and got the very best in materials and craftsmanship to make his dream a reality.

Having bought Trevena House and founded the Fellowship of the Knights of the Round Table in 1927, Glasscock ordered the walls and floors at the rear of the building to be removed. This created the space for a large hall, with an oak-finished barrel vaulted ceiling and a dais on which stands the Throne of King Arthur. Large paintings depicting the most dramatic episodes from Arthurian adventure fill the wall space. A *son et lumière*, avoiding computer-generated gimmickry and relying on simple lighting

and the stirring narration of actor Robert Powell, highlights the chief episodes of Arthur's life.

Beyond is the much larger Hall of Chivalry. Glasscock pronounced, when opening it in 1933, that it was built to 'perpetuate the immortal memory of Arthur, King of Britain, and to enable the Fellowship of the Knights of the Round Table of King Arthur to make better known the ideals of chivalry…'

The long Hall of Chivalry is hung with beautifully decorated flags and 125 finely carved granite shields. Whilst the near end is dominated by dark colours, the far end with its massive throne, surmounted by a huge canopy supported by nine granite pillars, is overtopped by a magnificent stained glass triptych, its light symbolically beckoning the visitor forward.

Veronica Whall created the stained glass windows (73 in all) which bathe the Hall in ever changing light and colour. It was the largest commission of her long artistic career. Like the rest of the ensemble, Whall's stained glass is rich in symbolism and has a strong Pre-Raphaelite inspiration.

Fore Street, Tintagel PL34 ODA, 01840 770526

Bude Watchtower

This tower is also known as the Pepper Pot because of its peculiar shape. It was built in 1835 for Sir Thomas Dyke Acland. Although it served as a shelter for the coastguard on their patrols, it was far grander and more ornate than mere practicalities demanded and may be regarded as a folly, or at least a piece of very good whimsy.

It was designed by George Wightwick of Plymouth and modelled after the Tower of Winds in Athens, which also provided inspiration for Beckford's Tower pages 37-8). With this classical reference, it comes as no surprise that Wightwick was the partner of John Foulston, who designed the Egyptian House and Devonport Town Hall (page 23) and later succeeded to Foulston's architectural practice.

Like the Temple of Winds, Bude's Watchtower is octagonal. However, its eight sides do not depict the eight deities of the winds like its Greek forebear, but are simply marked with the points of the compass carved below the cornice. Due to cliff erosion, it was re-sited in its present (very windy) position in 1900 – but 7 degrees off centre! It will need to be moved again before long. Look north for a great view of the Breakwater – built in 1819 and rebuilt in 1839 after storm damage – and Bude Haven.

Location: Compass Point on the Coast Path just west of Bude, SS199064

Devon

Hartland Folly

Standing proudly on Warren Cliff above Hartland Quay, Hartland Folly (SS 225253) – also known as the Pleasure House – remains something of a mystery. Easily accessed from the Coast Path, it is now partly ruinous and a large round-headed arch is its main feature. Among the signs of extensive alterations are traces of two windows, a fireplace on the second floor and a staircase.

The Department of the Environment in 1989 cautiously described Hartland Folly as 'possibly late 16th century in origin remodelled in the later 18th century'. It was first mentioned as the Pleasure House in a letter of 1738 and was first shown on an early 18th century map depicting nearby Hartland Abbey and its estate.

The Abbey, which is open to the public, stands a mile to the east in a much better chosen and well sheltered site in the Abbey River valley. Local author R Pearse Chope suggested that the magnificent arch dates from the time of Paul Orchard (1739-1812), who is said to have had the building altered so that he could back his carriage into it and enjoy the view, protected from wind and rain. Certainly Orchard's era was one when building artificial ruins and prospect towers amid dramatic scenery was fashionable. Furthermore, the exposed site of the Pleasure House is only really suited to a folly.

The Landmark, Ilfracombe

The Landmark Theatre stands in dramatic contrast to Ilfracombe's classic Victorian architecture, consisting of brick cones, constructed without formwork in the same way as 18th and 19th century kilns. Locally known as 'Madonna's Bra', the bold and unashamedly modern Landmark has also been compared to the cooling towers of a power station.

It was completed in 1998 for under £5 million, replacing the Pavilion Theatre, a Victorian building badly damaged by fire. As well as its 480 seat theatre, the Landmark houses the Tourist Information Centre, a 200 seat multi-purpose flat floor space, café bar, foyers and cinema facilities. The Landmark was voted one of the ten most significant buildings of the 1990s and has received many awards; it was chosen by the Arts Council, Royal Court and Theatres Trust for their case study about theatre design 'Building the Best'.

The Promenade, Ilfracombe EX34 9BZ   01271 316523

St Nicholas' Chapel, Ilfracombe

St Nicholas' Chapel, perched on Lantern Hill and overlooking the harbour and the Bristol Channel, is reputed to be Britain's oldest working lighthouse. There was a beacon on Lantern Hill to guide ships into the harbour even before St Nicholas Chapel was built there *c*1300-25.

The chapel was secularised at the Reformation and became a dwelling, but continued as a lighthouse. In the mid-19th century, John Davie was lighthouse keeper. He and his wife raised fourteen children in the chapel, which must have been a very tight squeeze. Now restored and open to the public, the Chapel continues as a lighthouse, its automatic navigation light being looked after by Ilfracombe's Harbour Master.

Occasional church services are also held at the Chapel, which has a good collection of Victorian photographs and press cuttings, as well as model ships, and offers a lovely view of the harbour.

Seasonal opening

Pack of Cards, Combe Martin

A Grade II* building, the Pack of Cards was erected as 'an everlasting monument to Lady Luck' by George Ley, the squire of Combe Martin, after he won handsomely at cards in 1690. The result might be called a practical folly. Based on a deck of 52 playing cards, the inn is 52 ft square with four storeys for the four suits. There are 52 windows and, prior to the window tax of 1696, the panes of glass in all the windows added up to the total of the numbered cards in a pack. Continuing the theme, there are 52 steps in the staircase, 13 doors on each floor and 13 fireplaces. The four chimneys in the top floor represent the four kings and the four chimneys below the four queens. The squire's study has 13 panes of glass and the joker window is incomplete.

The Leys continued to use the Pack as their family home for over a hundred years. It became an inn during the early 19th century – the list of landlords goes back to 1822 – when it was known (a bit unimaginatively) as the King's Arms. It gained the distinctive name Pack o' Cards officially in 1933.

High Street, Combe Martin EX34 0ET, 01271 882300

Rhenish Tower, Lynmouth

Lynmouth's 19th century 'Rhenish Tower' is something of a mystery. One authority claims it was a gift from a General Rawdon and a copy of the tower at Drachenfels in the Rhineland: 'Finding his aesthetic taste outraged by a naked iron water tank erected on posts, he built this pleasing feature to harmonise with the scenery.'

The Lynmouth tower does indeed look like the Drachenfels tower, and all things German were in vogue during Queen Victoria's reign: she and Prince Albert (from Coburg in the Rhineland) were frequent visitors to Germany. Although no Rawdons were recorded in the relevant Lynmouth censuses, Lt General John Dawson Rawdon, MP (1802-66) resided in London, but a probate of his will described him as also being 'of Lynmouth'.

If General Rawdon built the tower, when did he do so? The sources differ on this question, one claiming it originated in the 1820s or 1830s, others favouring 1855 to 1860. They also differ on whether Rawdon had any practical reasons to build the tower. It may have been to guide mariners and fishermen safely into harbour, which would explain the brazier on top of the tower, said to have been replaced later with an electric light with a range of ten miles. It has also been claimed that the tower's tank stored sea water for bracing indoor baths and that the water was pumped to the General's house, 'Clooneavin', high on the hill above Lynmouth Street. If this is the case, pumping water to such a height would have demanded great force.

The tower as it now is may differ from the original. Its balconies and machicolations are thought to have been added later in response to suggestions that it was an eyesore. Furthermore, the tower was rebuilt after the terrible floods of 1952, which devastated

Lynmouth and cost 34 lives. Whatever the exact truth, the Rhenish Tower, remains as a delightfully weird addition to Lynmouth's harbour.

Lynmouth Harbour, SS 723495

Watermouth Castle

Watermouth Castle is a country house built in 1825 with fine views of the north Devon coast. However, it was never entirely the conventional residence of local bigwigs: George Wightwick designed it to look like a castle with turrets and castellations, in much the same way as Sir Edwin Lutyens later designed Castle Drogo (page 25). Unlike Drogo, Watermouth now hosts a theme park (admission charges), offering to take visitors back to the simple pleasures of Victorian life with animated scenes, a model railway and musical instruments that play themselves. Other attractions include Gnomeland, a variety of rides, crazy golf, Soft Ball Shooting Canons and music from Captain Andy and his Dog Band.

Located on the A399 between Ilfracombe and Combe Martin at SS555480, EX34 9SL. (The exterior can be viewed from the road.) Seasonal opening. Contact 01271 867474

*Opposite:
Devonport Town
Hall and column*

*Left: The
Egyptian House,
Devonport*

*A detail from the
Egyptian House*

Egyptian House, Ker Street, Devonport

The Egyptian House was built in 1823 in the Egyptian style popular after Bonaparte's Egyptian campaign and Nelson's victory at the Battle of the Nile (1798). It formed a weird ensemble, along with the Grecian Town Hall and column and the now vanished 'Hindoo' chapel and Regency terraces – victims of the Luftwaffe and post-war planners respectively. The whole group was designed by John Foulston (1772-1841), a leading architect of the day. It

expressed Devonport's civic pride when it was still an independent town and arguably more important than neighbouring Plymouth.

The Egyptian House was originally built as a classical and mathematical school, and has served as a library, the meeting place of the Oddfellows Society, and a club. It has many interesting features, including its bulgy Egyptian columns and capitals, the windows with their tapering frames and patterned glazing. Egyptian motifs grace the stuccoed façade.

Grecian Town Hall, Ker Street, Devonport

Fulston's Grecian Town Hall is the centrepiece of Ker Street – an architectural gem well complemented by the neighbouring Greek Doric column. Its four column Doric portico has classical beauty and proportion. Rather weirdly, it is surmounted by the figure of Britannia – who was completely unknown to the classical world as her invention lay far in the future. No matter! She was modelled in Coade stone and added by J Panzetta in 1835, fourteen years after the hall itself was built.

Ker Street, Devonport PL1 4EJ

Highwayman Inn, Sourton

The Highwayman Inn is *very* weird. A cross between a fairy tale and an antiques shop, it is filled with the strange and singular. Enter through the stagecoach lobby – the genuine article, formed from one of the original coaches plying the Okehampton-Launceston road.

It's like entering Aladdin's Cave, full of lantern-lit nooks and crannies. There are swords and shields, a stag's head, horse brasses, blacksmith's bellows, church pews, sewing machines and Old Mother Hubbard's shoe. Even the bar is weird: hewn from Dartmoor bog oak, thousands of years old and pickled in acidic, peaty water.

Welsh boxer Buster Jones and his wife Rita bought this ancient coaching inn in 1961, and then set about scouring local auctions and farm sales, buying whatever took their fancy. This is their legacy, especially the Rita Jones Locker Bar. Filled with fittings from 19th century whaling ship Diana, including her oars and ship's wheel and lit by oil lamps slung from the ceiling, this bar has an atmosphere all its own. Reputedly, it is the most haunted part of the Highwayman....

On the A386 Okehampton-Tavistock road at Sourton, EX20 4HN
01837 861243

Castle Drogo

England's newest castle isn't really a castle at all, but an eccentric gentleman's residence. Standing 150 metres above the rocky Teign Gorge like a stage set from a Dracula movie, Castle Drogo was built between 1911 and 1930. Grocery tycoon Julius Drewe asked Sir Edwin Lutyens, the leading British architect of the time, to design it.

Drewe, who founded Home & Colonial Stores and grew so rich so fast he was able to retire at 32, had no wish to stint on 20th century comforts. He had two turbines built on the banks of the Teign to supply electricity for lights and lifts. Drogo's plumbing and central heating would have astonished medieval builders too, had they been able to travel through time to see the castle, though its huge blocks of granite masonry would have been just their choice.

Castle Drogo's arrow slits and castellations, its imposing gatehouse with its carved lion and Latin motto are a delight, but purely for show. No attempt was made to complete the medieval illusion within: inside it is a luxurious country house.

National Trust. 01647 433306. SX721900, EX6 6PB, signed from A382, 5 miles south of A30 Exeter-Okehampton road

Haldon Belvedere

Haldon Belvedere near Dunchideock is a cross between a memorial, a luxury residence and a folly. This triangular tower with its angle turrets and Gothic windows stands proudly on the crest of the Haldon Hills and is a landmark for many miles around.

Although often called 'Lawrence Castle' and dedicated to the father of the Indian Army, General Stringer Lawrence, it serves no military purpose whatsoever. It was built in 1788 by local boy made good, Sir Robert Palk, who made his pile in India – due in large part to his friend and patron, General Lawrence.

Palk rose rapidly, working for the East India Company, serving as Paymaster and Commissary to the Indian Army and later becoming Governor of Madras.

The childless General Lawrence spent his retirement as Palk's guest in nearby Haldon House (now demolished). When he died in 1775, he left the then massive sum of £50,000 to his host. Duly grateful, Palk spent some £2000-£3000 building the 26m (85ft) high Belvedere, which includes a life-sized statue of Lawrence dressed as a Roman general. Below are three large tablets describing Lawrence's career in glowing hyperbole.

We learn that Major General Stringer Lawrence commanded the British armies in India for twenty years and 'by his superior genius …established the Empire of Britain in Hindostan'. Not only this, but 'he aspired to and obtained a name more glorious than that of Conqueror. He was the Deliverer of India. At his approach every village poured forth its inhabitants … while blessings in different languages and from every side were showered on him.'

Take the Dunchideock turn from the A38, EX6 7QY   01392 833846

The House that Moved, Exeter

The House that Moved stood 90m distant, at Number 16 Edmund Street, until 1961, when it was jacked up, set on metal wheels and rolled on rails to its present position (see photo on page 28). Moving the entire 21 ton house was a major project and took six days to complete. Stripped to its frame, its windows removed, it was clad in ten tons of protective timber before it was winched slowly up the hill to the foot of West Street.

It is one of the oldest domestic timber-framed houses in Devon, thought to date from around 1450, and was originally called Merchant House. Although it had survived the Exeter Blitz, it stood right in the way of Exeter's planned inner by-pass and was scheduled for demolition along with many other historic buildings. Historians and archaeologists led protests for its preservation. At almost the last moment, it was listed and Exeter City Council's £10,000 contribution saved it from destruction.

24 West Street, Exeter EX1 1BA. Signposted from the city centre

Exeter Catacombs

The Catacombs are ostentatious tombs tucked away below street level in St Bartholomew's Cemetery. After a serious cholera outbreak in 1832 caused overcrowding in the neighbouring Bartholomew Yard burial ground, the Exeter Improvement Commissioners asked their Surveyor, Thomas Whitaker, to design a new cemetery on the steep slopes below. For the Catacombs, the most prestigious part of his design, Whitaker followed the vogue for things Egyptian - also seen in the Egyptian Houses in Devonport and Penzance (pages 3 and 22).

Although the Catacombs did not prove a dead loss, few people were lowered in their coffins on ropes to the vaults below – and these had prodigious capacity for the deceased, said to be 22,000. Most who found their last resting place at St Bartholomew's Cemetery were interred in (cheaper) common graves.

Bartholomew Street West, Exeter EX4 3AL

Fairlynch Museum, Budleigh Salterton

Fairlynch is a classic example of a *cottage orné* [ornamental cottage] and was built in 1811 for Matthew Yeates, a local ship owner and banker, when such fancy 'cottages' for the well-to-do were fashionable. Usually architect-designed, *cottages ornés* were play houses for the wealthy, not homes for working people. In contrast to the formality and strict proportions of the Georgian style, they cheerfully mixed a variety of influences, including rustic, Gothic, Tudor, Regency and neo-classical. Fairlynch has arched windows and Gothic glazing; these and the oval window over the porch and the belvedere above the roof are all decorative features not found in the plain and functional cob and thatch cottages typical of Devon.

Cottages ornés were part of the then new-found taste for the picturesque, popularised by Romantic poets such as William Wordsworth and painters including J M W Turner. They were mainly built in attractive West Country seaside towns, which could not easily be reached by working class people from London and the industrial cities – at least until the railway arrived. A la Ronde (page 32) is another fine example of the style and was originally thatched with white walls like Fairlynch. *Cottages ornés* can also be found in Sidmouth, Salcombe, Exmouth, Teignmouth and Lyme Regis – and, on a grander scale, at Endsleigh Cottage near Milton Abbot in the Tamar valley.

Fairlynch and its pretty garden are open during the season as a local history and geology museum and can at the time of writing be explored free of charge (donations please). It has a fine collection of rocks and fossils from the Jurassic Coast, as well as archaeological finds from prehistoric to recent times. There are special costume exhibitions, and a room devoted to local boy Sir Walter Raleigh, along with a large copy of The Boyhood of Raleigh, a famous Victorian painting by Sir John Everett Millais, who used Budleigh beach as the backdrop. Other rooms commemorate smuggler Jack Rattenbury from Beer and Vice-Admiral Preedy, who played a large part in laying the first Atlantic telegraph cable in 1858 and retired to Budleigh. Children's toys, the railway, medicine and education are also featured at Fairlynch.

27 Fore Street, Budleigh Salterton EX9 6NP   01395 442666
Seasonal opening

A La Ronde, Exmouth

This unique sixteen sided house with its diamond shaped windows was created around 1795 for two wealthy spinster cousins, Jane and Mary Parminter, who decorated it with seashells, feathers, seaweed and sand, lichens, stones, bones, cut paper and marbled paint. Their eclectic tastes in architecture, art and collecting had been greatly stimulated by their eleven years of travel through Europe – an extraordinary adventure for unaccompanied 18th century ladies, especially in times of war and revolution, but the Parminter cousins were remarkable women.

Jane and Mary spent many years decorating A la Ronde, where the wedge-shaped rooms are accessed from a central octagonal hall, which rises over thirty feet to the lantern roof and Shell Gallery in the apex of the roof. Their work is the most accomplished of its kind surviving in Britain, yet their technique was simple: they stuck feathers to card and attached this to the plaster surface. Shells and other materials were pressed into the lime putty skin before it set.

Time has exacted a toll on these delicate and intricate designs, but the National Trust has undertaken an extended programme of restoration. Visitors can no longer enter the Gallery, though they can view it in detail and from virtually every angle on CCTV screens. As the Trust has bought the surrounding land and saved it from development, the panoramic views across the Exe Estuary and the Haldon Hills remain as splendid as when Mary and Jane followed the sun on its course around their house. Mary survived her cousin by many years and stipulated in her will that A la Ronde and its contents be preserved intact and that only unmarried kinswomen might inherit it. However, a change in the property laws eventually allowed one male owner, who replaced the original thatched roof with tiles and greatly extended the living space by adding dormer windows to the attic and dividing it into rooms.

Summer Lane, Exmouth EX8 5BD, 01395 265514
Seasonal opening

Somerset

Ashley Combe Toll House

This curvaceous arched and thatched building on the Worthy Toll Road near Porlock Weir became a tollhouse in 1950. Dating from the late 19th century, it was formerly the lodge for Ashley Combe House, a mansion of 1799, demolished by 1974. This mansion was the home of Countess Ada Lovelace, a mathematician and computer pioneer and the only legitimate child of Lord Byron. Although Ada Lovelace is sometimes also credited with designing the tollhouse, this seems unlikely as she died in 1852.

The toll road winds downhill from Pit Combe Head on the A39 to Porlock Weir and is a gentle alternative to the notoriously steep Porlock Hill on the main road. It was probably built in the 1840s as a carriage drive and offers superb views of Porlock Bay.

1 mile west of Porlock Weir on the Worthy Toll Road at SS857484, TA24 8PG. Also accessible on foot via the Coast Path and the Coleridge Way. Please note this is a private house and respect the owners' privacy.

Dunster Yarn Market

Dunster's eight-sided Yarn Market is highly unusual if not unique and has dominated the main street since 1609. Wool and the cloth trade were the mainstay of Somerset and Devon's economies for centuries and local bigwig George Lutterell built the Yarn Market to shelter traders and channel wealth towards Dunster, where his family castle provided protection. The timber-framed Yarn Market is built around a central stone core and lean-to roof with strong beams and dormers. One of the beams has a hole in it, the result of cannon fire during the English Civil War when Dunster Castle was commanded by Colonel Wyndham for Charles I and endured five months' siege. Once there was a shambles (butchers' market) alongside the Yarn Market, but this is long gone.

High Street, Dunster TA24 6SF

Dunster dovecote

Dovecotes are most often found in the grounds of manor houses or monasteries. As pigeon houses they served a practical purpose – although they look bizarre to modern eyes. Before 'Turnip Townsend' introduced root crops for winter feed into England in the early 18th century, it was necessary to slaughter large numbers of sheep and cattle at Michaelmas and salt the flesh. Fresh meat

The Dunster dovecote is thought to be the only one in the world to have a revolving ladder in full working order and turning on a 400 year old bearing

was at a premium, but domestic pigeons, with their very short breeding cycle, could supply meat and eggs all the year round.

The Dunster dovecote is a fine example of its type, supplying the Castle up to 1870 and the Priory until its suppression in 1539. It was probably first built by the Norman Baron de Mohun, but later improved by Benedictine monks. They installed the revolving ladder to reach the nests, up to 6m (20ft) off the ground in the stone tower. The present ladder, built of ash, is some 400 years old and a replacement for an earlier ladder.

The dovecote lies behind Dunster's parish church and is open daily all year round.

Burnham Low Light

Mention 'lighthouses' and most people think of tall stripy towers with a lantern on top. That would be a fair description of Burnham-on-Sea's High Lighthouse – now decommissioned and let as holiday apartments. However, Burnham's lighthouse on legs defies expectations. Built of wood and standing on nine wooden piers, it is a modest 11 m (36 ft) high. It was built in conjunction with the High Lighthouse in 1832 to warn shipping of the exceptionally dangerous mud flats and rapid tides in the Bristol Channel, where the tidal range of 15 m (49 ft) is the second highest in the world, after Canada's Bay of Fundy.

Warning lights were pioneered in the 18th century by a Burnham fisherman's wife, who kept a candle burning in her cottage window to guide her husband and his friends home. Grateful sailors paid her small sums. Later, the Sexton gave her £5 for the right to place a light in the church tower. In his turn, the Sexton received £20 from Revd David Davies, who built Burnham's Round Tower, which originally had four storeys.

Davies was paid an exceedingly generous £12,000 compensation by Trinity House in 1829 to douse his light and make way for the High Light. This was built slightly inland, of traditional stone and brick, and stands an impressive 33.5m (110ft) tall.

Located at the northern end of Burnham's beach, ST 298503

Beckford's Tower

Beckford's neo-classical Italianate tower (photo on page 38) stands 47m (154ft) above Lansdown Hill near Bath. It was built in 1827 as a library and country retreat for the art collector, novelist, critic and slave-owner William Beckford, who is quoted as saying: 'So, I am growing rich, and mean to build towers.' He also built a series of pleasure gardens, 'Beckford's Ride', between the tower and his home in Lansdown Crescent.

Like the original owner, visitors today can enjoy magnificent views over the surrounding countryside from the belvedere at the top of the tower. This gilded lantern is based on the Temple of Vesta at Tivoli and the Tower of Winds at Athens. In retrospect, Beckford wished he had made the tower forty feet higher – though visitors hiking up the grand spiral staircase might not concur.

The museum collection at the base of the tower, which includes paintings, prints, *objets d'art* and furniture originally made for the tower, further expresses Beckford's wide ranging dilettante tastes.

Although parts of Beckford's Ride nearer Bath have been built over, the Tower Gardens remain in the form of a huge cemetery, the last resting place of over 5000 Bathonians. They include H E Goodridge, the architect of the tower, whilst Beckford himself resides under a monumental marble slab, isolated on its own island and surrounded by elaborate memorials.

Lansdown Road, Bath BA1 9BH. Open weekends and Bank Holiday Mondays in season. contact Landmark Trust, 01628 825925

Ralph Allen's Sham Castle, Bath

The Sham Castle is like a two dimensional stage set from a Monty Python sketch, but built in stone. Naturally, this was Bath Stone as it was erected by Cornishman Ralph Allen, who first transformed the postal service and then made his second fortune developing Bath's quarries, which provided the golden stone that helped make Georgian Bath a leading provincial centre and one of England's most beautiful cities.

Allen's Sham Castle was constructed in 1762 to improve the prospect from his Palladian mansion in Prior Park. Today, the view from there is blocked by houses, but at the time the façade of the Sham Castle with its towers and turrets, its arrow slits and castellations, would have looked convincing enough from that angle.

A closer inspection reveals it for what it is – a perfect folly from an age which delighted in building elaborate structures of limited or no practical value, often with a false historical flavour. The reverse side of the Sham Castle is simply a plain wall…but I feel rather a spoilsport in telling you that, and that the Sham Bridge at Ralph Allen's nearby Prior Park Landscape Garden (National Trust BA2 5AH, 01225 833422) is merely a screen at the end of the Serpentine Lake.

Access to the Sham Castle is via the Golf Course Road, but parking is limited there. More parking is available on North Road, which is linked to Golf Course Road via a footpath.

Some other weird structures

There are some structures which can't really be called 'buildings' but which are nevertheless equally weird. Here are two examples.

The Angel's Wings is a shelter with a wooden bench, built for Sir James Hamlyn as part of the Clovelly estate, probably in 1826.

And the monument to Sir Humphry Millet Grylls in Helston, Cornwall, was described by Sabine Baring-Gould as 'designed for execution in sugar-candy and carried out in granite'.